COSTUME AROUND THE WORLD
Mexico

Jane Bingham

CHELSEA CLUBHOUSE
An Imprint of Chelsea House Publishers

Produced for Chelsea Clubhouse by Bailey Publishing Associates Ltd
11a Woodlands, Hove BN3 6TJ
England

Project Manager: Roberta Bailey
Editor: Alex Woolf
Text Designer: Jane Hawkins
Picture Research: Roberta Bailey and Shelley Noronha

Chelsea Clubhouse
An imprint of Chelsea House Publishers
132 West 31st Street
New York NY 10001

ISBN 978-0-7910-9771-7

Library of Congress Cataloging-in-Publication Data
Costume around the world.—1st ed.
    v. cm.
    Includes bibliographical references and index.
    Contents: [1] China / Anne Rooney—[2] France / Kathy Elgin—[3] Germany / Cath Senker—[4] India / Kathy Elgin—[5] Italy / Kathy Elgin—[6] Japan / Jane Bingham—[7] Mexico / Jane Bingham—[8] Saudi Arabia / Cath Senker—[9] Spain / Kathy Elgin—[10] United States / Liz Gogerly.
    ISBN 978-0-7910-9765-6 (v. 1)—ISBN 978-0-7910-9766-3 (v. 2)—ISBN 978-0-7910-9767-0 (v. 3)—ISBN 978-0-7910-9768-7 (v. 4)—ISBN 978-0-7910-9769-4 (v. 5)—ISBN 978-0-7910-9770-0 (v. 6)—ISBN 978-0-7910-9771-7 (v. 7)—ISBN 978-0-7910-9773-1 (v. 8)— ISBN 978-0-7910-9772-4 (v. 9)—ISBN 978-0-7910-9774-8 (v. 10) 1. Clothing and dress—Juvenile literature.
    GT518.C67 2008
    391—dc22   2007042756

Printed and bound in Hong Kong

10 9 8 7 6 5 4 3 2 1

The publishers would like to thank the following for permission to reproduce their pictures:
Chris Fairclough Worldwide Ltd: 9 (Ed Parker).
Corbis: 18 (Danny Lehman).
Lupita Sosa: 17.
Topfoto: 4 (Rick Strange/AA), 5 (Image Works), 7 (The British Library/HIP), 8, 10 (Image Works), 11 (Charles Walker), 13, 14 (Rick Strange/AA), 15 (Spectrum/HIP), 16 (Image Works), 19 (Image Works), 22 (Image Works), 23 (Image Works), 24 (Image Works), 25, 26 (Longhurst), 27 (Dallas John Heaton), 29 (PA Photos).
Topfoto (RCS/Alinari Archives Management, Florence): 6, 12, 20, 21.
WETA: 28.

Contents

Mexico and Its Costumes

The country of Mexico lies directly south of the United States. It has thousands of miles of coastline but also deserts, mountains, and rain forests. Many parts of Mexico are wild and isolated, but its capital, Mexico City, is one of the world's most crowded cities.

Different people

Mexico has a rich mix of people. The earliest people to live in the region were Native Americans, also known as indigenous people. Today the descendants of these native people still live in Mexico. They belong to many different groups, and each group has its own traditions and costumes.

In Mexico's cities, people usually wear Western-style clothes, like their neighbors in the United States.

Many Mexicans have a Spanish heritage. They are descended from Spanish settlers who arrived in Mexico from the early 1500s on. They brought Spanish customs, culture, and dress to Mexico.

Today many Mexicans are mestizos—people whose ancestors are a mix of indigenous and Spanish. People from different parts of the world have also come to live in Mexico. Together all these people have created a rich blend of traditions.

Different costumes

Each area of Mexico has its own traditional costumes. Many of these costumes have an ancient native history. Others show strong Spanish influences. But whatever their history, Mexican costumes are famous for their brilliant colors and stunning patterns.

Color from insects

One of the most common colors found in Mexican costumes is a vivid crimson. In the past, this color was made by crushing the bodies of tiny cochineal insects that live on cactus plants. Today textile makers in Mexico often use chemical dyes, but some cochineal dye is still produced from insects.

Mexicans love to dress up in their traditional costumes for dances and festivals.

Mexico Past and Present

The first major civilization in Mexico was established around 1200 BCE by the Olmecs. They were a warlike people with powerful rulers and priests, and they set a pattern for a long line of native civilizations.

Early civilizations

The Olmecs were followed by the people of Teotihuacán and then by the Maya, who flourished between 300 BCE and 900 CE. Most Mayan people dressed in simple tunics, but Mayan rulers and priests wore huge feather headdresses and golden chest ornaments.

After the Maya, the Toltecs rose to power. Then in the 1340s, the Aztecs began to build an empire. The Aztecs had a powerful army led by warrior knights dressed as jaguars and eagles.

These Mexican dancers are dressed like their Mayan ancestors, in dramatic headdresses and costumes.

Spanish rule

In 1521, a Spanish army arrived in Mexico, and within a few years they had captured all the Aztec lands. For the next 300 years, Mexico was ruled by Spain. Millions of Spanish settlers came to Mexico bringing their religion, language, customs, and costumes.

Spanish-speaking men in Mexico wore simple cotton pants and shirts for work and close-fitting pants and short jackets for special occasions. Women usually wore full skirts, blouses, and shawls.

An independent nation

In 1821, Mexico won its independence from Spain, but this war was followed by many other conflicts. Today many Mexicans are extremely poor, while others have a similar lifestyle to their neighbors in the United States.

These days, poor people in country areas still tend to wear traditional clothes, influenced by native or Spanish styles. In contrast, city dwellers—both rich and poor—usually wear American-style clothes.

An artist's view of Spanish soldiers arriving in Mexico. The contrast between the costumes of the Spanish soldiers and the Aztec warriors is very strong.

Fancy fashions

When the Spanish conquerors arrived in Mexico, the native people were astonished by the way the Spaniards dressed and wore their hair. They created comic masks showing Spanish gentlemen with pointed beards and fine lace collars.

A Land of Contrasts

The Mexican countryside is highly varied. In the north are vast stretches of desert, while the southern part of the country is covered by tropical rain forest. There are flat, swampy plains beside the coast and massive mountain ranges farther inland. Most Mexicans live in the central highlands—a high, rocky region surrounded by mountain peaks.

A varied climate

In Mexico's desert regions, it is very hot and dry, but the temperature drops dramatically at night. During the day, people wear light clothing and wide, shady sombreros. At night, the men keep warm by wearing a serape—a woven poncho with a hole for the head. Women wrap themselves in shawls.

In the central highlands, the days are usually warm, but it can be cold in winter. People

In the colder parts of Mexico, people wear serapes or shawls for warmth and sombreros for protection from the sun.

usually wear several layers of clothing and a hat or scarf to shade them from the sun. The southern parts of Mexico are hot and steamy, so people dress very simply. They may wear a traditional, loose cotton tunic or American-style light summer clothes.

Useful materials

Farmers in Mexico have been growing cotton since Mayan times, and this is still the main material used for clothes. Then in the 1500s, Spanish settlers began to bring sheep and cows to Mexico and wool and leather became important materials too. Wool is used for weaving warm clothes, and calfskin is made into belts, sandals, and boots. Sometimes whole suits are made from soft suede leather.

Cotton and cactus

In the Aztec Empire, only rulers and nobles were allowed to wear cotton. The ordinary people had to wear clothes made from cactus or other plant fibers. Today cactus fibers are used for embroidering patterns on leather clothes.

A Mexican farmer in the hot and steamy south, wearing American-style, lightweight cotton clothes.

Religion and Culture

Mexico does not have an official religion, but many Mexicans belong to the Roman Catholic Church. The Mexican people also have a very long history of native beliefs, which are remembered in dances and festivals.

Catholic festivals

Roman Catholics in Mexico hold many festivals to mark holy days. At these festivals, people walk through the streets in processions, priests wear finely embroidered robes, and everybody dresses in his or her best clothes. Women usually wear crosses and rosaries around their necks.

The largest Catholic festival is the Feast of the Virgin of Guadalupe. Children all over Mexico dress up in traditional dress and visit churches. Little girls wear colorful necklaces, embroidered tunics, skirts, and patterned

Children from northwest Mexico dress in traditional costumes for the Feast of the Virgin of Guadalupe.

shawls. Boys wear serapes, or ponchos, and sandals and paint mustaches on their faces. On their backs, the children carry wooden frames with examples of Mexican crafts hanging from them, such as tiny clay pots.

Ancient dances

Today many Mexicans still perform dances to keep their ancient traditions alive. They wear traditional masks or dress up in the costumes of their distant ancestors. In the mountains of northwest Mexico, people perform a deer dance. Dancers wear headdresses to represent a sacred deer and the cruel hunting dogs.

La Danza Azteca is performed at festivals in many parts of Mexico. In this spectacular war dance, men carry feather shields and wear feathered headdresses just like ancient Aztec warriors.

The Day of the Dead

The Day of the Dead is a Christian festival, but it also has an older origin, in the native ceremonies for honoring dead ancestors. On the Day of the Dead, people make models of skeletons. Some people wear masks and dress up as skeletons, tigers, or bats.

This dramatic costume is being worn for a parade on the Day of the Dead.

Textiles and Weaving

These days, Mexican clothes are made from a wide range of modern textiles, but traditional clothes are still usually made from cotton or wool. The wool or cotton thread is dyed vivid colors and woven into cloth following traditional patterns. Many traditional garments are decorated with embroidered patterns, especially around the neck.

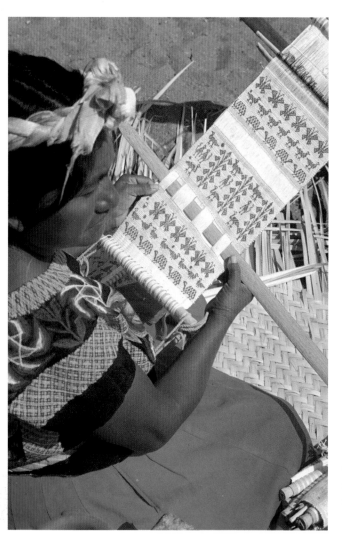

A woman from the southern coast weaves traditional patterns on a back-strap loom.

Back-strap looms

In remote country areas, women still weave their cloth on a back-strap loom. These simple looms have been used in Mexico since Mayan times. The loom is tied at one end to a tree and the other end is fixed to the weaver's belt. This allows the kneeling weaver to control the tension of the threads.

Back-strap looms produce long, thin strips of cloth that are sewn together to make traditional garments such as the *huipil*, a straight tunic with a hole for the head.

Weaving patterns

Each region of Mexico has its own distinctive weaving patterns. For example, weavers from the Saltillo area, in the northwest, produce garments with colorful rainbow stripes, while the Chiapas weavers, from southeast Mexico, are famous for their striking geometric designs.

Every weaving pattern has its own ancient meanings. In the weaving of the Chiapas people, a scorpion represents a prayer for rain and a diamond symbolizes the world.

Here are some colorful examples of Chiapas weaving. Local rain forest birds often feature in the Chiapas patterns.

Weaving for the saints

In some parts of Mexico, people weave special clothes for the statues of the saints. Each generation of weavers makes a new set of clothes for the saint, copying the patterns used in the old garments. Through this tradition, the ancient patterns are kept alive from one generation to the next.

Traditional Dress

The style of Mexican traditional dress can vary greatly from one region to the next, but there are a few basic garments that make up a traditional Mexican costume.

Many Mexican men wear a large straw sombrero and a striped serape over their pants and shirt.

Men's traditions

Mexican men have two basic types of traditional costume. One is usually kept for everyday wear, while the other is worn on special occasions.

For everyday wear, many Mexican men wear loose cotton pants and a tunic or shirt, which is sometimes tied with a colorful sash. In cold weather, this basic outfit is covered by a woven serape, or poncho. On their feet, men wear leather sandals or boots, and their head is covered by a wide-brimmed sombrero made from palm leaves.

For festivals and formal occasions, men often wear a stylish fitted outfit, copied from the *charro* outfit worn by Mexican cowboys (see pages 18–19). This outfit is worn with boots and a fancy sombrero made from palm leaves or felt.

Decorating sombreros

In some Mexican villages, men decorate their sombreros using ribbons, feathers, beaded bands, or colorful pom-poms. Sometimes they even hang beer bottle lids from the brims of their sombreros!

Women's traditions

Mexican women's costumes can vary greatly in style. In the southeast and in other areas with strong native traditions, women wear a simple cotton tunic called a *huipil* and a wraparound skirt. In other parts of the country, where the Spanish influence is stronger, women wear a long-sleeved, embroidered blouse and a full, flounced skirt. Women all over Mexico cover their arms and shoulders with a large, rectangular shawl.

These girls are wearing colorful *huipils* and sashes—the traditional native costume of Mexico.

15

Clothes for Special Occasions

Many Mexicans wear a version of their traditional costume for special events, such as weddings and funerals. Men wear an elegant *charro*-style outfit (see pages 18–19) and women wear their finest embroidered clothes and shawls. People also dress up for festivals and dances.

Mexican hat dance

The Mexican hat dance is the national dance of Mexico, and it is performed on many public occasions. The dance tells a story of love and courtship, and it involves a lot of twirling and stamping. For the dance, the men wear a *charro*-style outfit and a very large sombrero. The women have dresses with very full skirts and often wear the China Poblana (see page 17). During the dance, the sombrero is thrown high into the air, and the dance ends with the couple kissing behind the hat.

Dancers perform the Mexican hat dance. When the women swirl around, the effect is dazzling.

China Poblana

The China Poblana comes from the Puebla region of Mexico. It has a full red-and-green skirt decorated with beads and other ornaments, an embroidered short-sleeved blouse, and a brightly colored sash.

Like many Mexican costumes, the China Poblana has a striking combination of patterns.

According to a Mexican legend, the China Poblana was named after a Chinese princess who was kidnapped by pirates in the 1600s. The princess was sold in a Mexican slave market and lived for many years in the Puebla region. There she dressed in a special style that combined both Chinese and Puebla elements.

Hats from baby clothes

For special occasions on the Isthmus of Tehuantepec, women wear a wide, lacy white headdress called a *huipil grande*. According to legend, this garment was copied from baby clothes that were washed ashore from a Spanish shipwreck. The local women thought the clothes were head shawls and turned them into beautiful, elaborate hats.

17

Clothes for Men

Most Mexican men today wear American-style clothes. But if they want to look really stylish, many of them still dress up in a *charro*-style outfit.

Charro outfits

The *charro* outfit dates to the time of the early Spanish settlers, when wealthy landowners wore elegant riding costumes made in southern Spain.

These tight-fitting outfits were made from black velvet or soft doeskin. They had narrow pants and a short bolero-style jacket. The jacket was fastened with silver clasps, and a row of silver buttons ran down the outside seams of the pants.

With the *charro* outfit, men wore a loose white shirt decorated with embroidery and a flowing bow tie. The outfit was completed by boots with silver spurs and a wide-brimmed felt hat called a *chapeta*.

For special occasions, such as weddings, Mexican men and boys often dress up in their *charro* outfits.

Mexican musicians wearing the *traje de mariachi*—a simpler version of the *charro* outfit.

Copying the *charros*

By the 17th century, *charro* outfits had become the special dress of the Mexican cowboys (see page 22). However, in the early 1900s, a simpler version of the outfit was adopted by Mexican musicians. These outfits are often known as *traje de mariachi*, or musicians' outfits. Unlike the true *charro* outfits, they come in a range of colors and have cheap buttons and clasps made from brass. The *traje de mariachi* swiftly became popular with ordinary Mexicans.

Ceremonial costume

A very stylish version of the *charro* outfit is worn for grand ceremonies and banquets. Known as *traje de ceremonia*, this dark *charro* outfit has silver buttons connected by chains down the outside pant leg and a set of brooches fastening the jacket. Black patent leather boots and a silver-plated revolver in a holster complete this formal outfit.

Clothes for Women

Mexico's cities are full of young women in Western-style clothes, but some older women still wear traditional dress—especially those who live in the country. Often women combine Western-style clothes with a traditional garment, such as a *huipil* or a shawl.

These women from southwest Mexico are wearing a colorful variety of *huipils* and simple skirts.

Huipils

The *huipil* has its origins in the cotton tunics worn by the Maya and Aztecs. It is made from a rectangle of woven cotton cloth with

a hole left in the center for the head. The garment is then folded in half and the sides stitched up, leaving a gap to allow for armholes. *Huipils* are often embroidered with traditional patterns.

Skirts, sashes, and shawls

With their *huipil*, women usually wear a simple wraparound cotton skirt, which is tied at the waist with a colorful sash. In regions where the Spanish influence is stronger, women wear an embroidered blouse instead of a *huipil* and a full, flounced skirt.

Most Mexican women wear a shawl. This useful garment is often wrapped around the upper body and tucked into a sash. In the mountainous regions of southeast Mexico, the shawl is a simple woven rectangle of cloth called a *tzute*. In other parts of the country, women wear a *rebozo*—a larger shawl that often has long fringes at each end.

A thick cotton *rebozo* makes a strong and cozy baby carrier.

Useful rebozos

The *rebozo* can act as a sling for a baby and as a carrier for wood or other objects. The women of Oaxaca, in southern Mexico, wear their *rebozos* twisted over their foreheads with one end hanging down their backs. They wrap this end around their heads to help them balance a jar on their heads.

Clothes for Work

In Mexico today, T-shirts, shorts, or jeans are common work wear for men, while women at work often wear a simple cotton dress. However, in country areas, people still wear traditional clothes for work.

Mexican cowboys

Mexican cattle herders—known as *charros*—usually wear a rugged version of the *charro* outfit (see page 18). Sometimes they also wear extra goatskin coverings over their pants, known as chaps. The serape (or poncho) is an important part of their work clothes. It is very practical for horseback riding and can also be used to sleep in at night.

Cattle herders often wear loose shirts and ties without a jacket. The man in the front of the picture has leather chaps covering his pants.

Useful belts

Many Mexican farmers wear a useful belt called a *mecapal*. It is made from a wide strip of leather or woven cloth, with ends that are joined together by a cord. When a man has a load to carry, the cord is used to secure the bundle on his shoulders and the strip is placed over his head.

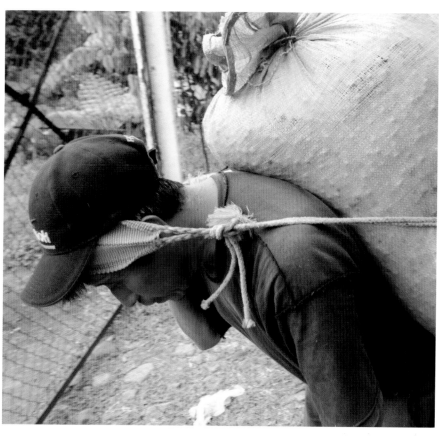

A farmer uses a *mecapal* to carry a heavy sack.

Uniforms

Mexican firefighters, doctors, and nurses have very similar uniforms to the ones worn in the United States. Today the Mexican police also dress in modern uniforms. However, in the 1860s, a mounted police force called the *rurales* was formed in Mexico. The *rurales* wore a gray *charro* outfit braided in silver, a wide sombrero, and crossed belts over their chest to hold a sword, rifle, and pistol. The *rurales* continued to wear their distinctive uniforms until the early 20th century. They have been described as the world's most picturesque policemen.

Car tire shoes

Mexicans traditionally wore leather sandals to work. But recently, rubber sandals made from old car tires have become popular. The thick tread make them very good at gripping the ground.

Clothes for Sports and Leisure

When they want to relax, Mexicans wear casual clothes, such as jeans and sweat suits, just like people all over the world. When they are playing sports, they wear modern, international sportswear. However, there is one traditional Mexican sport where people dress up in amazing costumes. This is the *charreada*—or Mexican rodeo.

A *charreada* rider is dressed for action in his soft, wool suit.

Dressing for the *charreada*

At the *charreada*, male and female riders show off their skills at handling horses and herding cattle. It is a very exciting display, and all the competitors dress up to look their best.

Male competitors wear very fancy *charro* outfits made from suede or soft, cashmere wool. The suits often have suede shapes stitched onto them using a method called appliqué. They are also covered in embroidered patterns in silver, gold, or cactus thread.

Women riders

Women riders in the *charreada* wear long skirts and ride sidesaddle. Some of them wear a female version of the *charro* outfit with a long, full skirt, and some wear a dress called an Adelita.

The Adelita is a Spanish-style dress with a very wide skirt, long, puffed sleeves, and a wide sash. The dress is named after a legendary woman soldier who fought in the Mexican Revolution.

On their heads, both men and women riders wear a sombrero made from felt or palm leaves and decorated with embroidery. The sombrero has a high, stiffened crown to protect the riders' heads if they fall.

A colorful Adelita, worn with a darker shawl.

Soccer style

Mexicans are wild about soccer. Many Mexican boys wear the Mexico team colors of green and white. When they are going to matches, some Mexico supporters wear the team colors plus a large sombrero with the word MEXICO painted on it.

Important Extras

Mexicans don't just wear brilliant, colorful clothes—they also have great accessories. Women decorate their hair with flowers, ribbons, and combs, and men add extra details to their sombreros. Mexicans are also very fond of jewelry.

Ancient ornaments

The Mexicans have a long history of jewelry making. As early as the 1000 BCE, the Maya were making large pectorals (chest ornaments) from beaten gold and pendants and ornaments from pieces of jade. Later the Aztec nobles wore golden necklaces, armlets, and anklets as well as nose plugs and earplugs made from gold and precious stones.

Mexican silver

Today many Mexicans wear silver jewelry—especially rings and earrings. Mexican silver jewelry is often inlaid with pieces of turquoise or shiny abalone shell, and silversmiths also

A stunning display of Mexican silver jewelry.

specialize in a filigree technique in which tiny silver threads are twisted together to make a pattern. Crescent-shaped earrings called *arracadas* are especially popular.

Other accessories

The type of accessories people wear varies from region to region. The Huichol people of western Mexico wear necklaces, headbands, belts, and bags made from tiny, colorful glass beads. In Chiapas, in southeast Mexico, pieces of amber are tied around children's necks to protect them from harm. In the central region of Taxco, tortoiseshell from the hawksbill turtle is used to make elaborate hair combs carved in the shape of horses, crocodiles, or mermaids.

Mexicans have a flair for putting all sorts of colors together!

Bags for all

Mexican men and women often carry a simple shoulder bag called a *morral*. These bags are woven from cotton or wool and are large enough to carry groceries or books.

International Style

The person who did the most to promote Mexican style was Frida Kahlo. She was a young Mexican artist who wore traditional clothes in a very stylish way.

When Frida visited New York in the 1930s, people were amazed by her dramatic clothes with their vivid patterns and colors. Photographs of Frida were published in *Vogue* magazine and started a trend for Mexican clothes.

In 2002, a movie about Frida Kahlo's life was released, with the part of Frida played by Salma Hayek. The movie created a new wave of interest in Mexican textiles and patterns.

The artist Frida Kahlo introduced Mexican style to the United States and to the wider world.

Mexican trends

Some Mexican garments have become very popular in Europe and the United States. Embroidered tunics and blouses, full, flounced skirts, and even ponchos have been popular fashion items in the last few years.

Recently, some European and American women have started wearing *rebozos*. These traditional Mexican shawls are used by some young mothers in place of manufactured baby carriers because they are seen as a more natural way to carry a baby.

Recently, some top designers have turned the Mexican poncho into a fashion item.

Dramatic jewelry

Frida Kahlo did not just start a trend for Mexican clothes. When a photo of her hand with a ring on every finger was seen in *Vogue* magazine, chunky Mexican jewelry was suddenly in fashion. Now Mexican jewelry is worn in many parts of the world.

Glossary

Adelita A Spanish-style dress with a very wide skirt, long, puffed sleeves, and an enormous bow and sash.

appliqué A method of decorating cloth by stitching shapes of another fabric onto the cloth.

arracadas Crescent-shaped, silver Mexican earrings.

Aztecs An indigenous American people who lived in Mexico from the 1300s to the 1500s.

back-strap loom A simple loom that is tied at one end to a tree while the other end is fixed to the weaver's belt.

bolero A short, fitted jacket that ends just above the waist.

cashmere A fine, soft wool made from goats' hair.

chapeta A wide-brimmed felt hat.

chaps Leather leggings worn by cowboys. Chaps cover the fronts and sides of the rider's pants but have no seat.

charreada A Mexican rodeo, in which riders show off their skills at handling horses and herding cattle.

charro **outfit** A tight-fitting outfit with narrow pants and a short jacket decorated with clasps and buttons.

China Poblana A colorful, full-skirted dress, worn with an embroidered blouse and a wide sash.

filigree Very delicate metalwork made from twisting together metal threads.

flounced Decorated by gathered ruffles of material sewn onto the garment.

huipil A traditional straight tunic worn by Mexican men and women.

huipil grande A wide, lacy, white headdress worn by some Mexican women.

indigenous Belonging to a region or native to that region.

isthmus A narrow strip of land connecting two large land areas.

Maya An indigenous Mexican people who flourished between 300 BCE and 900 CE.

mecapal A belt worn by Mexican farmers that can also be used as a carrying bag.

mestizos Mexicans whose ancestors are a mix of indigenous American and Spanish.

Mexican Revolution A period of conflict lasting from 1910 to 1921 when ordinary Mexican people fought for their rights.

morral A simple shoulder bag woven from cotton or wool and used by Mexican men and women.

Olmecs An indigenous American people who lived in Mexico from about 1200 to 400 BCE.

rebozo A large shawl worn by Mexican women and girls. *Rebozos* often have long fringes at both ends.

rosary A string of beads used by some Christians to help them pray.

serape A kind of cloak made from a rectangle of cloth with a hole in its center for the head.

sombrero A felt or straw hat with a wide brim worn by men in Mexico.

Teotihuacán A city that flourished in Mexico from about 100 BCE to 600 CE.

Toltecs An indigenous American people who lived in Mexico between about 1000 and 1200 CE.

traje de ceremonia A very formal version of the *charro* outfit worn for grand ceremonies and banquets.

traje de maraichi A simple version of the *charro* outfit mainly worn by musicians.

tzute A simple, woven rectangle of cloth worn as a shawl by some Mexican women.

Further Information

Books

Heinrichs, Ann. *True Books: Mexico*. Children's Press, 1997.

Lewis, Elizabeth. *World Art and Culture: Mexican Art and Culture*. Raintree, 2003.

Parker, Edward. *Changing Face of: Mexico*. Raintree, 2002.

Stalcup, Ann. *Crafts of the World: Mayan Weaving: A Living Tradition*. PowerKids Press, 2003.

Web sites

www.mayanculture.com/materials.html
An illustrated guide to the textiles and clothing of the Chiapas people of southeast Mexico.

www.museumoftheamericanwest.org/explore/exhibits/charreria.html
A history of the *charro* outfit and other items of Mexican costume.

www.mexicantextiles.com/flies/thecollection.html
A collection of photographs of Mexican costumes and textiles.

Index